W9-CEH-239

Curious Creatures
BATS

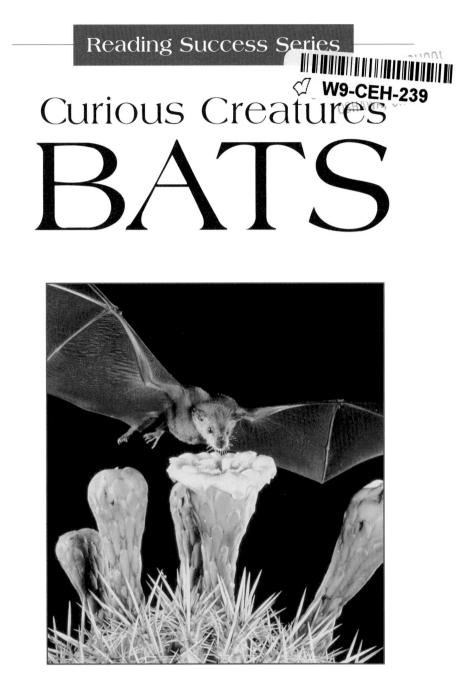

James Robert Taris
Louis James Taris

CURRICULUM ASSOCIATES®, Inc.

Editor: Joan F. Krensky

Designer: Jamie L. Ruh

Illustration Credits:

Jamie L. Ruh/pages 5 and 9

Photography Credits:

Merlin D. Tuttle/Bat Conservation International/
Photo Researchers, Inc./pages 1, 4, 10, 12, 15, and cover

Wolfgang Bayer/Bruce Coleman/Picture Network International, Ltd./
page 3

Gary Braasch/Tony Stone/Picture Network International, Ltd./page 6

Stephen Dalton/Bat Conservation International/
Photo Researchers, Inc./pages 7 and 11

Michael P. Fogden/Bruce Coleman/Picture Network International, Ltd./
page 8

J. Scott Altenbach and Merlin D. Tuttle/Bat Conservation
International/Photo Researchers, Inc./page 10

Art Wolfe/Tony Stone/Picture Network International, Ltd./page 13

Russ Kinne/Comstock/page 13

Phil Degginger/Bruce Coleman/Picture Network International, Ltd./
page 14

Many people do not like bats. Bats scare them. But bats are really interesting animals. Once people know more about bats, they usually stop being afraid of them. They may even get to like them.

Bats are **mammals.** They are **warm-blooded** and
fur covers their body. Like all young mammals, baby
bats are born alive and get milk from their mothers.
Bats are different from other mammals, though.
They are the only mammal that can fly.

Bats have strong wings and can stay up in the air for a long time. Although bats fly much as birds do, their wings are very different. Bats do not have feathers. Their wings are made from a thin layer of skin stretched over long bones. Each wing has two arm bones and five finger bones.

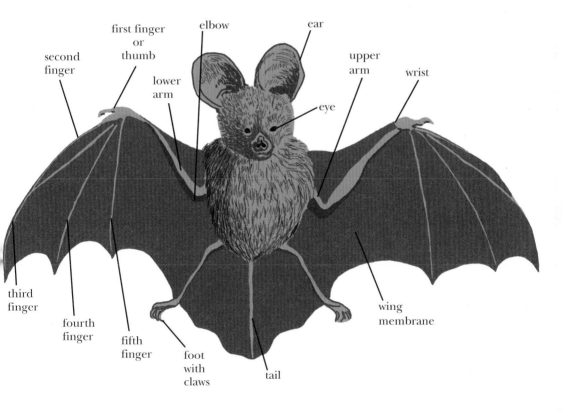

Most bats sleep during the day. They usually rest, or **roost,** in dark places. Bats make their homes in caves, mines, tunnels, buildings, and trees. When bats are resting, they usually hang upside down. They use their sharp toe claws as hooks. Sometimes bats squeeze into cracks between big rocks or walls, or hide behind the loose bark of trees.

At night, bats fly off in
search of food. Most bats
feed on insects. They mainly
eat **mosquitoes.** A bat can eat
as many as 650 mosquitoes
in one night.

There is a saying "as blind as a bat." Bats are not really blind. Most bats, however, have tiny eyes that cannot see very well in the dark. They don't use their eyes to hunt and find their way. They use their ears.

yellow-winged brown bat

Bats make high squeaking noises as they hunt for food. These sounds spread out through the air like waves. When the sounds hit an object, they bounce back as echoes. The bats' large ears easily pick up the echo sounds. By using this **echolocation,** bats can find insects at night without bumping into trees and walls.

Not all bats feed on insects. Many bats eat fruit. Other bats drink the sweet liquid, or **nectar,** from flowers. Some bats catch fish. There are even bats that feed on the blood of other mammals. This kind of bat is called a vampire bat.

Vampire bats live in Central and South America. They mostly attack farm animals such as cows, pigs, and horses. Usually a vampire bat lands on a sleeping animal and bites the animal's skin with sharp front teeth. When the cut bleeds, the bat drinks the blood.

vampire bat

Most bats are gentle creatures. Unless they are trapped or frightened, they won't bite people. Vampire bats, though, sometimes attack people sleeping outdoors. People in areas where vampire bats live must protect themselves. Some vampire bats carry a dangerous disease called **rabies.** The vampire bat may pass on this disease with its bite.

Altogether there are about 1,000 different kinds of bats. They live all over the world, but they like warm places best. Bats come in many sizes. The smallest bats are about the size of a bee. Their open wings spread about five inches. The biggest bats have a **wingspan** of five feet.

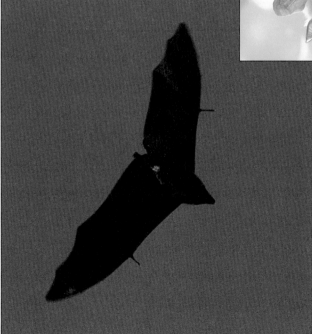

The fruit bat is one of the world's largest bats.

In North America, one of the most common bats is the little brown bat. It is almost four inches long and has a wingspan of about eight inches. The little brown bat hunts insects at night and spends its day resting in dark caves, hollow trees, and buildings. Like most other bats, little brown bats live in large groups, or **colonies.** Some colonies may have thousands or even millions of bats.

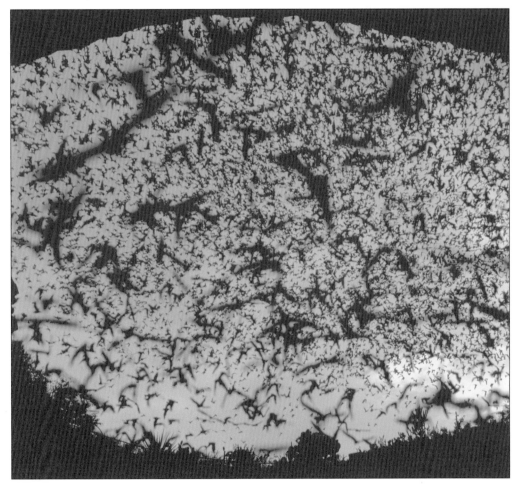

a bat colony flying out of a cave

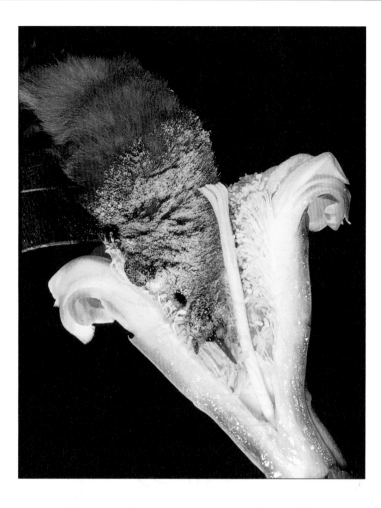

Bats are important to **ecology.** They help keep down the number of insect pests. They carry **pollen** from one flower to another. Their **droppings** are used to help plants grow. Although bats are nature's helpers, some people treat them as enemies. People kill bats or destroy the places where they live.

In China, some people wear a special **charm** on a chain around their neck. The charm is a circle of bats connected wing tip to wing tip. The Chinese people believe that bats bring good luck. More people need to understand that bats do good.